CrossRhodes

Lindsey F. Rhodes

Creative Talents Unleashed

GENERAL INFORMATION

CrossRhodes

1st Edition: 2014

Publisher Information

1st Edition: Creative Talents Unleashed
CreativeTalentsUnleashed@aol.com
www.ctupublishinggroup.com

ISBN-13: 978-0-9905009-1-9
ISBN-10: 10:0990500918

Dedication

I dedicate this book to my parents and siblings. Also, to anyone in the universe whom I met along the way on this journey called Life. Also I would like to thank the following people for encouraging me to write on: Sarah Easter, Elgin Pierre, Lionel Irons, Leo Williams, Anthony McGraw, Raja Williams, Sharon Goodwyn, Drea Yeya, Sandra Smith, and Vickie Erwin. To those who I may have forgotten, blame it on the brain and not the heart. Though our time here is limited; we still have to make the most of it and grab opportunity and life by the horns.

"We all have dreams. But in order to make dreams come into reality, it takes an awful lot of determination, dedication, self-discipline, and effort." Jesse Owens

Preface

Hardships and triumphs are the peaks and valleys that are encountered in life. We rise like the sun daily hoping to redeem ourselves from the previous day. Going through the same rigmarole without taking time to appreciate the simpler things in life, time is often taken for granted and flies by without us even knowing it. Contented are we with the routine without questioning it and what is the purpose of living?

This journey began in 1995 when I started to take an appreciation to the literary arts. What started out as an outlet to alleviate tension became a passionate way to voice an opinion. Though the course was deviated along the way, I still managed to maintain the drive to press forward in this newfound venture. I was drawn to write through life's experiences using both current and past events. Speaking out through a different perspective and using poetry as an outlet to convey that very message.

In the summer of 2005, my family and I were forced to leave my hometown of New Orleans, Louisiana due to Hurricane Katrina. A catastrophic event that was detrimental to my soul at that time. It was a very difficult experience and also a challenge to get adjusted to a new state, town, and a new culture that was foreign to me. We were embraced as family and curiosity was often the focal point of conversation. While society was asking me questions about where I am from, I was searching for answers and what was my purpose here.

In the fall of 2010, I decided to have the courage to share my poetry with the world. Being five years removed from that horrific summer of 2005, I was finally settling in a new life in Appalachia. Initially I joined a local poetry group which I did not take seriously in all honesty. I became lazy from a creative standpoint. I shared my thoughts with a few friends in social media and in essence they were telling me to "just put it out there". I haven't looked back since then.

In short, I will be sharing my tales on all sorts of subject matter with a mix of personal struggles and triumphs. I am now in southern Ohio and let's just say I am still adjusting to the culture but it is a welcome change of pace from before. I approach everything with two caveats in mind, Listen and Consider. Welcome to my journey, the CrossRhodes.

"A reading man and woman is a ready man and woman but a writing man and woman are exact." ~ Marcus Garvey

Lindsey F. Rhodes

"There are moments in our lives where we find ourselves at a crossroads. The choices we make in those moments can define the rest of our days. And, of course when faced with the unknown, most of us prefer to turn around and go back."
- Lucas Scott

Table of Contents

Table of Contents . . . continued

xi

Table of Contents . . . continued

Table of Contents . . . continued

Epilogue

CrossRhodes

Lindsey F. Rhodes

Creative Talents Unleashed

Surreal Life

Chief architect of emotional roller-coasters whose tumultuous ride
Got me feeling all tingly inside
Stinging sensation of a true infatuation
Staring through the depths of the soul; providing mental stimulation
Opportunities I began to realize, observing the prize
That many fail to recognize
Making initial contact while onlookers despise
Crossing a line that few can define
A landmark of elegance that is simply divine
Complimenting it with sweet nothings while losing a sense of thinking
By doing spontaneous things that are quite scintillating
After a moment of clarity knowing the Life isn't to fair to me through witnessing illusions
Not being able to draw conclusions everything is not what it seems
I am trying to accept the fact that this is just another dream.

S.E.L.F.I.E.
(Self -Egotistical Live False Image Enhancement)

Expressing of ideals that aren't up to par
Daydreaming of being a shining star
Always living in the absolute
Believing in the lies that is passed off as the truth
Stretching at arm's length to catch a peek
Posing as a wannabe while perpetrating as the meek
Alone in the world yearning for attention
Unexplained actions that are beyond comprehension
Enriched with a false sense of security
Smiling for the camera is the only surety
To escape from a fractured reality
Removing the veil so I can have some clarity

2 Cents

Garment of emotions covering the skin
Heartless and thoughtlessness; when will the misery end?
Makes me want to just scream and holler
Penny for my thoughts must equate to a dollar
And not enough cents to make sense of it all
Appointed by the heart only to see it fall
Sun setting on this chapter
Weakness seemed to be the blinders; caught up in this
rapture
No need for any sort of sympathy
Diatribe fallen on deaf ears; no love for me
Was fully vested but now I'm mentally broke
Opportunity that's just gone up in smoke
Situation is getting critical and somewhat dire
In search to quench the fire of someone's desire

Lindsey F. Rhodes

Skin Deep

Happily melanated
Deciding the fate...be incarcerated or educated
Should I be proud to enter this institution?
Born into a fraudulent reality; sparking a revolution
Striving to play the game on an unleveled playing field
Enticed by "scholarships",room, and board just to sweeten
the deal
Restricted by roadblocks to obtain financial aid
Plastered our faces on pamphlets to serve as a Band-Aid
To conceal the deep scars embedded within
Exploited and abused in all aspects because of the hue of
my skin

Stunted Growth

Neglected and discarded like yesterday's garbage
Witness to domestic conflicts and profane verbiage
A small wonder lost in an expansive world
In need of guidance; just ready to swirl
Out of control while being confined
Dumpster as my bed and boxes as my pillow is all I can find
Appetite for destruction and infatuated with the streets
Laying low for survival while law enforcement do their daily sweeps
Anger and an occasional sneer are my costumes to mask the pain
Readying for redemption; yearning to be home again
Grown up now both physically and mentally
A recent graduate from Adversity University
Preparing for the future making it quite clearer
Gazing through the windshield and not the rearview mirror

Chasing the Dragon

It was love at first sight
First encounter occurred in the dimmest of light
Lips made love for the first time to this newfound stranger
Consequences were forthcoming for one was facing
imminent danger
Braggadocios about an out of body experience
Time ticking away on finding her were getting serious
Anger and hostility served as the backdrop for desperation
From robbing to stealing; anything just to refit into her
equation
Finally after countless efforts he got the chance to meet her
again
Not as sweet as the first time; for he felt a sharp pain
Stemming from the heart that was hardened by bad choices
Living a life of regrets by listening to the wrong voices

Matchstick Men

Moment of silence for commenced to reading
While the innocents are begging and pleading
Panicking at calamity's disco searching for a safe haven
Freedom and questions needed answered is all they were
craving
From being chased and tormented for initiating queries
To following false trails to "conspiracy theories"
The revolution was televised, but the channel was turned
Baring witness to the carnage while the edifices burned
Dire consequences for spreading the real truth
Dwelling in the garden of good and evil ingesting strange
fruit

The De-Valuation

Anticipation has its foothold
Fleeing from this captivity that seems to never grow old
Ranting and ranting in trying to escape
Anxious to express the mind before it is too late
Intuition seems to be distant at this point
Dealing with a power struggle....who to anoint?

Obvious signs of dissension that cannot be seen
Following blind leaders to one's demise...what does it
mean?

Their teachings are merely exaggerated pulp fiction
Reach out and enlighten instead of causing friction
Unite and rise against a divided front
Toleration of ignorance is what they seem to want
Hell on earth awaited the timid that chose not to be blunt

Liberty is a Crackhead

Gone are the days of the universal collective
Blinded by false ambition; ever changing her perspective
Strung out are her people in need of a fix
Polluting, poisoning, and murdering the innocents just for
kicks
Serving as collateral damage in the name of greed
Adrenaline pumping through unconventional rituals to feed
the need
Of a "better" place to escape from the norm
Oblivious to the fact of an incoming s**t storm
Insatiable appetite for that alluring taste
No regard for consequences thus actions are in haste
Ostracizing her peers for fear of criticism
Yearning to be the center of attention wherein lies the great
schism
Between good and evil for the meek shall inherit
Her damaged goods but at what price does it merit?

No Apologies Needed

False indoctrination
To rampant and widespread incarceration
For the sake of population control
Taxing on the psyche as well as the soul
What happened to the doers, believers, and dreamers?
Transformed to murderers, haters, and schemers
Lost our way to a point of being despondent
Once an independent culture now chemically dependent
On money, sex, vices and various drugs
Adorned in tattoos, sagging pants to the repeated mantra
"We are thugs!"
Standing room only on the journey ahead
Yearning for simple things like water, freedom, and bread
What does the future entails for us all?
Without unity we are deemed to fall

Dear Justice

Dear Justice,

You are a selfish son of a b***h
Punishing the less informed to glorifying the snitch
Depart from the ones that are in dire need
To satisfying the soul that yearns for greed
Profiling in stereotypical fashion
Stirring the pot of ignorance waiting to just cash in
Always making a point to mention the "originators"
Slanted propagandists media being broadcast while playing
the part of the instigators
Providing lie-awyers at one's disposal and renting them out
like Avis
Where were you for individuals such as Jordan Miles,
Oscar Grant, and Troy Davis?

Sincerely,
Anonymous

Dis-Connect I.C.U.T.

Going through the motions
Curtailed by daily stress and mounting emotions
Monumental facade as far as the youth are concerned
Slowly maintaining the bridge before it is burned
Glimpse into the future as it appears to be bleak
Tragedy after tragedy; the heart becomes weak
For it is only temporary; caught up in the circus
Blinded by negative imagery with no defined purpose
To dream is to be crazy and noncompliant
Digital demons live and streaming in HD seems to be
dominant
Caring for those only in times of convenience
Maintaining the status quo; adhering to obedience
For fear of losing it all
Journeying to a fabled fiscal cliff with nothing to break the
fall
False unity throughout the community while praying for
change
An age old equation only through a new set of eyes is the
only way to rearrange

Requiem of a Celebrity

Gone are the days of being a kid
Waiting with anticipation by the phone for the next gig
Armed with determination with dreams and hope
Overbearing parents figuring ways to cope
With newfound exposure for all to view
Naïve to it all with no inkling of a clue
Front and center not ready for the world's judgmental
attitude
Concealed within the internal torment that is beginning to
brood
Temptation has become the go to friend
Reckless abandonment to no end
Wear and tear eroding the psyche
Posed with the same question…why does anybody want to
be like me?

Flippin' Da Script

Lights, camera, action.
Another bank bailout.....oh it's just another transaction
Who can't seem to get any satisfaction?
The writing and passing of new edicts in order to gain some traction
Cerebral goons forming global factions
By having caste systems broken down like fractions
We are like traffic lights; under social cooperation
Blinded and unknowingly misinformed with no visualization
Places everybody for a change is to occur
It will be instantaneous event in a blur
Chaos and panic will soon ensue
For one who speaks in opposition; nightmares will become true
Closely monitored and tagged like cattle
Put on the make up for this will be an uphill battle
Lives will soon unravel
Confined to four walls and no semblance of vision; no need for travel
Keep one's mind occupied with a propagandist spiel
In due time the cast will reveal A set of guidelines a contingency plan
..............And Cut!! It's in the can

TBD (The Black Diaspora)

Lo and behold the originators `
Harmonious by nature until the inception of the instigators
Seething from envy waiting to stir the pot
Stripped of dignity and "rights" seem to be the intricate plot
Scarred and stained to last a lifetime
What is the price-tag for such a heinous crime?
Change this change that implement this implement that
Crammed like sardines in an impromptu journey of a new
habitat
Trouble approaching asking for a dance
M-16 vision anticipating in a b-boy stance
Forever comforted by the ancestral spirits
Journey through life and still see the footprints

Animal Planet

Global stress
Third degree scars with no progress
Waiting for the kingdom to crumble
Striving to remain upright and not tumble
Off balance seem to be the stance
Tempted by the d'evils; shall we dance
Lulled to sleep with multimedia that's very hypnotic
On the brink of it all; tag and label them as psychotic
Engaging in the commerce of water
Whistling while remaining inattentive to both domestic and
foreign slaughter
At the turn of a corner scrutiny ensues while undergoing
surveillance
Get up stand up and evacuate Hope Island if one wants to
have a chance

Look Around

Winds of change
Swiriing about marching to a different beat wanting to rearrange
On how the status quo think
But the suits and ties will not blink
To help the common man or woman for the matter
Live streaming via HD is the pacifist's chitter chatter
Oblivious to it all; prepping for the next brand of entertainment
Common sense is on trial yet waiting for progress during a time of arraignment
Silence those who speak out against the machine
Covert cover to those individuals never to be seen
Or heard from again purging their existence
Do for self instead of relying on their assistance
This comes with a catch 22
The moment is at hand.....what the **** will you do?

Mistaken Identity

Constant interruptions of a harmonious culture
Swooping in with environmental waste; a tasteless vulture
Angry, irate and rightfully defiant
Gunshots and handcuffs greet you for being non-compliant
Peacekeepers armed with street sweepers
Laying waste to the wailers and the weepers
Sticks and stones brought to gunfights
Broken families abound to inexplicable plights
Irrational actions through calculating fear
For something rotten dwelled the water that full of waste
that was nuclear

Mud Cookies

Self-sufficiency in order to stay alive
Resorting to unconventional methods in order to survive
Neglected and "adopted" by ways of being objectified
Turning a blind eye knowingly for reasons that are not
justified
Desperate cries for help, hunger pains that are very
unforgiving
Sky high are food prices, plates of rice too rich for the slum
living
Earthquakes and civil unrest leading to unwarranted stress
Simplicity gone in favor of global complexity to see who
the best is
Hole in hearts yet no sympathy, does one not witness the
hurt?
Young children resorting to "cookies" made from butter,
salt, and dirt.

Excuse Me

I beg your pardon
Caught in the garden
Of Eden
A bit hesitant about leaving
But I won't because I am having a blast
How long will this happiness last
Conceal the scars and other wounds with tattoos
Subjected to unwritten laws and various taboos while the
ex-singing the blues
Spreading ill rumors as an accomplice to her misery
Trying her best to preserve a memory
Of a false reality that is no longer true to form
Heart is at ease now but is still in reform

The Illusionist's Dance

Struck down with an unnerving affliction
Resorting to any means to feed her addiction
Encountering roadblocks that is impeding the progress
Hedonism in the forefront of stress
Vision cloudy but praying for some rain
Lavish thoughts to conceal the pain
From the exploitation and abuse
Expressing the soul; letting it loose
Appeasing the audience through the plastic smile and
gyrations
Easing the mind off of turbulent situations
Made a covenant with the devil
To achieve greatness on any level
Onlookers ogling whispers showered with blank
compliments
All about them dollars with no sense

Slick Talk

Sun scorched soul anticipating the next catch
Nets are in place to bring in the next batch
A promise is comfort to a fool
Pacify the naive as if they are tools
Promised gold but were offered lead
Collateral damage amongst all leaving the hopeless dead
Livelihood that has been around for centuries
Goodbye to culture farewell to an industry
Curious onlookers searching for answers and asking
questions
Living the hard knock life and learning painful lessons
The sky has cleared and it is mostly sunny
Future is looking cloudy; now where is the money?

T.R.A.Y.V.O.N M.A.R.T.I.N.

Tragic event unfolding
Ray of sunlight fading while the elderly are scolding
Against the wind for such an atrocity
Yearning for justice that is just an outside possibility
Visions clouded by the copious amounts of coverage
Only the wicked looks in jest for any sort of leverage
Naysayers and supporters arguing over the nonessentials

Muddy are the waters with opinions; not questioning the credentials
Another day passes in search of renewed hope
Readying for the verdict; how will the masses cope?
Tempers are either soothed or flared
In anticipation for celebration or disappointment; the sides often glared
Now is the time for clarity where the real truth is bared

Coded Language

Simply misunderstanding
Classified and labeling through self-branding
This for this, that for that
24 hr. surveillance on where your head at
Clearance sale on your information
Filed under a G-14 classification
Shrouded in secrecy for the sake of support
Clouded by the underbrush; the adversary awaits in this
blood sport
Fueled by the fear mongers
Once considered allies are now the conquerors
Apocalyptic visions dancing in the head
Yesterday is history yet tomorrow is the mystery they seem
to dread
Masters of cryptic metaphors
Unwarranted in kicking the doors
Of the oppressed
Has a nation stressed
Trying to calm it
By harming it
How long will the mind take to figure out to decode and
detach
Doublespeak hitting the airwaves; another seed of
negativity just hatched

American Gangster

Flossing and profiling with their shiny suits
Smooth operators selling strange fruits
Armed with lawyers and a thick wallet
To vast real estate properties and a sexy starlet
Pinky and the brain mentality in wanting to take over the
world
While spreading lies and various propagandas to every boy
and girl
For how long will the veil conceal the true intentions?
Gobbling each of their words that are full of false
pretensions
Follow their own rules while changing them accordingly
Slowly liquidating the world starting with you and me
Advantageous over social ills
Taking what little is left to pay one's expense bills
The truth will reveal itself layer by layer
When it comes to global monopoly, I am not a player

F.E.D. U.P.

Screw all the elitists who try to defeat us
Keeping us behind bars like shell-toed adidas
Eugenics, the new extraction
Depletion of the masses and ideals through cultural
subtraction
Undivided attention to the mainstream
Relegated to a nightmare while pursuing "the dream"
Prophesizing about the final hour
Cleansing the nation with a blood shower
Yearning for change yet clinging to the past
Breaking news...another false flag attack; now the world is
aghast

Passing the Plate

Dressed to the nines in the finest attire
Belted out spirituals to take you higher
Jumping and stomping until you perspire
Singing a sing-a-long with the choir
Giving testimonials discussing a tempestuous life that was
prior
Mind and body as one setting the soul on fire
Riches and blessings is what is desired
Contributing to the "building fund" is what is required
Spoon-fed the illusion playing the part of the pacifier
Unaware of what will transpire
With this new sense of awareness
Miss-stepping intellectually remaining careless
Carrying you off to the nuthouse like Mariah
Forever being known as a pariah

Shampoo and Conditioner

Pointless propaganda with the cerebral cortex being
lathered
On with the shows that are on television while the sheep
are being gathered
Whatever happens to reading, writing, and arithmetic skills
that were vital?
Quick to rattle off all of the Kardashians to knowing who
won American Idol
Rinsing out the righteous teaching and entering the age of
ignorance
Multiethnic devils making dollars while we don't make any
sense
Is an era gone that was once full of promise and
prominence?
A super poligrip on the psyche and pulse of the world while
maintaining dominance
Trained to awake on a daily just to run in the rat race
All while maintaining a closed mind and staying in one's
place
Awed and infatuated by the latest trend, gossip, or tweet
The truth can be bitter going down to those whose appetite
for destruction was once accustomed to the sweet meat

Black, Blue, and Yellow

Premeditated often predicated on animalistic instinct
Nature of the beast attack first; asking questions is how
they think
Maintaining within the realms of the "law"
The trio was plain-clothed and all ready to draw
Cold hearted souls approaching like the winter in January
Without warning employing force that was unnecessary
An honor student laying to waste behind Mountain dew
Pigs running rampant donned in yellow leaving their
carnage black and blue
Ambush in the night literally kicked to the curb
Compensated and acquitted is how they do in the 'burg
Before putting on the mask of laughter and smiles
Take a minute and ask yourself where the justice for Mr.
Jordan Miles

Lindsey F. Rhodes

The G.O.O.D. Life

Toes on the line readying for the rat race
Conformity is emphasized for all to remain in place
Frivolous spending all in the name of credit
While exhausting a lifetime forever indebted
40-40 vision but cannot see the finish line
Conveyor belt movements; always on the grind
All of this hard work with nothing to show for it
Only to grow old and be knee deep in the s**t
The temple is crumbling on the brink of stressing out
Posing the question that will never be answered; "Where is
our bailout?"

House Rules

Punch the clock just to earn a wage
Locking up righteous ones confined into a cage
From pre-maturation to the elderly; forever a slave
With little or nothing left to bury but an empty soul in a grave
The expiration date on humanity is being accelerated
Random deaths that is inexplicable; often controlling and calculated
Drowning in the deep of the cesspool called debt
While lost souls stare into the wind as they constantly wept
The game is ongoing with no means to an end
Only to find out that the money is missing and one cannot cash in
The light is feint yet it is starting to come on
Enough of the chitter-chatter; time to take some cerebral and physical action

Renewal

Opportunity was sent knocking on desperation's door
Thinking subconsciously if there is more
Out there than ever before
Searching for fragments of fragility on the floor
Curiosity has become the navigational guide
Should these feelings be tested or just plain subside
Faith was chosen over fear for this latest adventure
Journey with the mind, body, and soul unaware on where it will venture
To or how long will it last the process moving quite slow but the heart is moving quite fast
On the road to redeeming this was thought to be forever lost
Greeted by optimism with a price; wondering how much did it cost?

Black Roses

A beautiful tragedy damaging mahogany in the making
Heightened voices interjects the soul into rhythmic shaking
Inanimate objects and fantastic dreams are suddenly the
new found companions from lighters to knives to a gun is
what one is brandishing
Violent interludes offset by sporadic praises
Intimidated by swift kicks, clenched fists, and arm raises
Spoon fed sweet lies to feed the complacent appetite
Second guessing occurs with the anticipation of hindsight
Thirst for normalcy, starving for love and peace
Body talk getting louder but the mouth remains steadfast
without giving a piece of the righteous mind which leads to
both physical and mental scars
Still yearning to be amongst the stars
Here lies a lovely woman who was both chattel property
and a slave
Embedded by black roses to conceal the tombstone upon
the grave

Sour Notes

Circa '79 a movement surfacing from the underground
Rhythmic four beat counts emerging with this new sound
Boom boxes, graffiti, tagging, to that b-boy stance
Countless battles ensuing on who was the best at break-
dance
Consciousness was at its apex
Fighting the powers that be; what will come next
Various cliques and factions always seem to be clashing
Gold medallions, chains and trendy fashions is what they
were flashing
Turn on the radio and what is heard now
Hot sex served on a platter, nice whips, to taking a vow
On corrupting young minds that is convoluted
To sampling of soulful sounds that are heavily diluted
Prospects awaiting their turn just to get in
Ask yourself; is it worth it in the end?

Silent Trumpet

The revolution will not be televised
Vices of a man that was well publicized
Old school wisdom through social commentary
To take heed or not to heed; results may vary
At a time when the world was in a tailspin
While it was cool to be proud of one's black skin
Crossing all cultures and various barriers
While questioning who will survive in America
Professing the truth in time of civil unrest
Armed with red, black, and green; ready to protest
A constant internal war with demons didn't seem to stop
Rest in peace to the godfather of hip-hop

Lindsey F. Rhodes

Hindsight

Inner crowd reject
Coy in a search for that future prospect
Self-imposed exile
Blurred from tragedy; armed with a melancholic smile
Chinks in the armor; the dropping of the veil
Satisfaction needs to be attained; time to exhale
Another contestant in the game of life
Peaks and valleys to triumph and strife
Manifesting to sanity and still asking questions
Still being steered into many directions with complicated
lessons

Alphabet Soup

Archenemies armed anticipating
Battling besieging berating
Counterfeit capitalism coinciding commercialism
Dire desire doing due diligence despotism
Egotistical enigmatic erroneously elected
Flawed fantasies facetious frauds fabricated
Genocidal governmental guerilla goons
Hustling hellishly hard holding high-tech harpoons
Indirect indecent individuals idling ideology idolizing
Juggling jargon jawing jerks jocking
Knowledgeable knuckleheads kidnapping killing
Legitimate loopholes logically lackluster
Misinterpreted messages morons must muster
Nonsensical news nagging the nameless
Oath occurring objectifying observing oppressors' that's
obvious
Parasitic path past purgatory pacifying
Quieting quizzical quoters questioning and quantifying
Rogue rebels revealing a ravaging regime
Savages stirring a senseless secular scheme
Taxing tyrants televising terrorism and taboo
Unilateral unions unconsciously undue
Vindictive visceral vying for validity
Watching warmongers wailing wildly
X-ray scanners observing us all
Youth running amok disrespecting the elderly et al
Zany zealots zeroing in on us with their gall

Coming to Terms

Enigmatic are the garment of emotions she would wear
Cut in on her spiritual dance if you dare
Full of dreams and aspirations
Temptation dwelling within the subconscious through the
trials and tribulations
Calculating ways to escape from the past
Unbeknownst that time was borrowed; how long will it last
An emotional train wreck hidden in plain sight
Undeterred by the odds; not giving up without a fight
Now an angel with wings preparing to fly
A precious life cut short without saying goodbye

Photo Booth

Readying for a timeless image and self-pride
Uncertainty setting in throughout this roller-coaster ride
Preoccupied with heinous thoughts and self-doubt
Questioning what this is all to do about
Waiting for the negatives to develop
The beginning of the great façade envelops
Into a grand lie established from the onset
Stones casted and thrown at glass houses; sorry for the disrespect
Reconciliation through kiss and make up
But patience is runneth over like the proverbial cup
A thousand words couldn't describe this Dark Age
For we were both actors playing our part out on society's stage

Lindsey F. Rhodes

Final Destination

Awaken with an epiphany
Hungry for knowledge; no breakfast at Tiffany's
Emancipation from the gross animation
Of slanted propaganda and mass media manipulation
Common sense along with a dash of non-compliance
Coming together and forming a dangerous alliance
Against the fractured establishment
Known for broken promises and embellishment
Karma's train is set to arrive
For the wise who excel and the vigilant willing to survive

Drifting Away

Building sandcastles that are on display
Oblivious to it all remaining intoxicated all day
Worshipping and paying homage to inanimate objects
Running of the gossip mill, politics, religion, and sports
amongst the many subjects
Temptation seems to be looming with each choice made
Should one gain notoriety or just plain fade?
Materialism and consumerism completes this dysfunctional
family
No sense of awareness in this not so complex calamity
What happened to respect of elders and sense of
community
Peace and family should be the chief priority

Exit

Love was the passenger in life's back seat
Needle to my soundtrack is stuck on repeat
So many options to choose from; yet no one is willing to
compete
Bombarded with problems; i dare to be discreet
Wandering about the boulevard of broken dreams
The ripping apart of a fragile soul from its seams
Too many thoughts to write down; going through reams
Of paper thinking of more unconventional schemes
Should I just give up and even concede
Defeat is not in the cards; this thought is to recede
In the back of my mind begging and eventually plead
That Change will soon come as this heart cease to bleed
Happiness...the next exit; caution is shall I proceed

Poker Face

Holding most of the cards to determine one's fate
Water-boarding, interrogation, and brutality is what awaits
at the gate
Badgers and pigs running rampant throughout the street
While genocidal acts abound and remaining discreet
The republic is still standing yet remains on life support
Hunters hunting the hunted for the sake of sport
Poisoning the well, to the dusting of crops
Phantom adversaries to the inception of photo-shop photo
ops
Misinformation is shown all over the place
Playing the cards in plain sight in the midst of a well-
dressed poker face

Bad Investment

Hopes, aspirations, and dreams were sold
Broken promises was what was told
Heavily invested with the heart as currency
All the eggs were in one basket; lost all of it both
emotionally and physically
Fatal missteps hinging on the brain
Scorched from being burnt while praying for rain
Tapped out with no inkling of hope
Going through the motions; how can one cope?
A seller's market searching for the right prospect
Stagnated at the moment; time to change the subject

Fool's Gold

Window shopping for love until cupid shot me in the arm
A preconceived breath of fresh air; infatuated by its charm
Floored by its presence; wanted to investigate
Too nervous in approach and too scared to initiate
Months after chasing and finally pursuing the ghost
I became the parasite and my new found friend; the host
Spell casted begins to wear off with misery rearing its ugly
head striving my head above water; should I continue to
tolerate or be dead?
dreams shattered for tempting fate
dwelling on the wouldas,
shouldas, and couldas but it was too late
Invested all my eggs into one basket
but will only receive flowers when I am in the casket
Glanced up into the sky wondering why,
Not being to myself by harboring an eternal lie

First Take

Armed with mind games
Altering both mental and digital frames
Questioning everything is it us or is it them
Actors and actresses in place assigned with a pseudonym
Impromptu cue cards ever changing the script
Sending freedom fighters and righteous teachers to their
crypt
Passive souls just playing spectators
The all black brigade inciting riots; call them the
aggravators
The entire world is a stage
At the point of no return with pent up rage
Risking freedom to be confined in a cage
Stuck on the same chapter; now let's turn the page

The Unraveling

Reopening a wound that still seems so fresh
The mind, body, and soul along with sanity still trying to mesh
Wrong place and wrong time
Caught in the crossfire at the scene of the crime
Upbeat attitude deflated by false accusation
Finding myself in a delicate situation
Heart lumped in my throat ready to scream damn it all
Elongated shadow and my conscious were the only witnesses to my potential downfall
Newfound enemies approaching me through inquiries unbeknownst to me
Praying for a miracle so my feet did the talking and I began to flee
Without any particular purpose
Until the truth finally surfaced
As a giant weight was being lifted off my back
That was the queue to get on track
Revenge was now the motive to redeem a fractured soul
Heightened anxiety and third degree stress began to takes its toll
14 years later and I still find myself wanting to flashback
Forever remaining focused and sharp as a tack
Wanted to take heed and adhere to the golden rule
One tough lesson that I had to endure in attending Life's school

Zombie Land

Seamlessly cavalier while remaining unaware
Cross the velvet rope if you dare
Preoccupation seem to be the vocation
Mental sabbaticals through submissive subliminal;
daydreaming taking that extended vacation
Worrying and stressing about the unnecessary
The soother and the comforter is the real adversary
Too many locks and not enough doors
That is not opened due to walking on egg-shelled floors
Liquidating all finances and preparing for that rapture
Tunnel vision to agony soulless ready for capture

Damaged Goods

So now the thrill is gone
Doped up, drugged up with death on the horizon;
destination the twilight zone
Piss poor, broke, and hopeless
So in love with misery;
Unscrupulous acts is what she commits
Pacifying tactics while telling her people to relax
Naïve to her monumental collapse
Her children running amok remaining destitute
Exhausted, overused, and exploited like an old prostitute
Covert affairs with her neighbors and all
Bearing false witnesses and specializes in the downfall
Of them while they look in dismay
Imperialism is on the rise; who is the next to fall prey?
Conform or die can be a daunting task
Layers and layers are being removed to reveal who is
behind the mask

Fatal Beauty

The meek and the feeble struggling to unearth that jewel
In lands far away; it is being purchased by the average fool
Deprived by lack of food and water
A hard day's work still couldn't produce a quarter
Fussing and fighting with one another to get ahead
Any sign of rebellion means that one will soon be dead
Homeland raped and pillaged for all its worth
Shackles unseen to the human eye ever since birth
Physically broken but the liberated spirit maintains the
wisdom
Blood, sweat, and tears poured out as the costs to pay to
attain freedom

G.O.O.G.L.E.

Inputting of data to search for lost souls
Masses are mere passengers while the unseen helm the controls
Latitude, longitude to topographical terrain
To instant gratification for those too complacent to complain
Copious amounts of information at the fingertips
For loose lips are sure to sink bureaucratic money ships
No matter where one lives or where one comes from
Exercise in nonconformity can lead to a violent maelstrom
Ladies and gentlemen for the time has come to reveal and uplift the veil
For suppression can no longer prevail
Intelligence over ignorance for the few
Open the eyes for one can spot a clue
Caution in the use of cerebral techniques for the search of justice can hurt you

Sponsored by Uncle

Blood sweat and tears
Only to return with post traumatic fears
Gone and come back forgotten
Chess pieces in their places while the players are plotting
Genetically modified propaganda is what is being force fed
Starvation abounds; may I have some water and bread
instead?
Infighting occurring with so much drama
Boys and girls displaced yelling for their mama
Wielding guns for their own defense
Along to die a martyr making no damn sense
Time to wake up and lace up the boots
By cleansing the mind and stop ingesting strange fruits

Running Faucet

Spewing running out of control
Can't seem to stop it; it is taking its toll
Drowned in the deceit and flooded by the truth
Poisoned the tree; where is the good fruit
Plot against the revolutionaries for breaking the silence
Incarcerate and incite the vicious cycle of violence
Wrongfully accused and trumped with charges
The veil is becoming transparent for the voices barges
In at an uncontrollable rate
Can't get them all....would love to determine their fate

Lindsey F. Rhodes

Just Friends

Chance encounter
Screaming that I finally found you
Singing sour notes of doubts; was this meant to be?
Or this was a little too much to take in
To being so much more than a friend
Is this a fantasy or a mirage of reality?
Questions that are confronted with on a daily
Distant memories of a faint smile
Under different circumstances now; just to go that extra
mile
Opportunity knocks but refuse to open the door
For the fear of déjà vu like countless times before
At the end of the tunnel and finally seeing the light
Blinded by the fact that you are a star shining bright
In essence letting go and just be free
The question was finally answered; this was meant to be

Randomonium

Scratching the surface like psoriasis
Yet 85 percent don't understand this
On why everything is materialistic
Dressing up the pigs to the tens with lipstick
Illusion of inclusion just to fit in
Judged by the melanin and other darken skin
Individuals who living through the struggle
Single parent two jobs having amongst other things to
juggle
Quick to judge the book by its cover
Infinite knowledge right here that is yet to be discovered
All in all shall be the beginning and the end
Broke like a project elevator; no money to spend
Head held high through perseverance
Self-sufficient are we; no need for interference

Lindsey F. Rhodes

A Plea for Bobo

There I lay in an open casket
Sending a message from the afterlife to the pathetic
ba****d
Who tortured and maimed me upon hearsay
All the while hoping the situation will eventually go away
Growing up without a father figure
Surrounded by unfamiliar town folk who only know me by
"n****r"
Here I lay 5'4 150 pounds with a stocky frame
Years later the rules of engagement still remains the same
All in all my death was not in vain
For the tables are still tilted; the scars and the chains remain

Epilogue

Lindsey F. Rhodes

About the Author

Sometimes the smallest step in the right direction ends up being the biggest step of your life. This is the very attitude that Mr. Lindsey F. Rhodes takes when it comes to new opportunities in life. Lindsey enjoys connecting with people through humor and life lessons. He has had the honor of serving his country and earning a college education.

Lindsey is the father of two beautiful children and raised four others from childhood. He is often asked how he can raise that many kids under the same roof and his response has always been "Time Management." His large family keeps his life interesting and thus in turn, a dull moment is never out of reach.

Lindsey enjoys reading, traveling, and learning new things that he can put into a poetic perspective. For him this is only the beginning of the journey.

Lindsey's Links

FaceBook

https://www.facebook.com/lf.rhodesii

Writing Group

https://www.facebook.com/groups/WritersConnection/

Author Page

http://www.ctupublishinggroup.com/lindsey-f.-rhodes.html

Creative Talents Unleashed

Creative Talents Unleashed is a publishing group that offers an inspiring platform for both new and seasoned writers to tap into and participate with. We offer daily writing prompts and challenges to fuel the writer's mind, a variety of writing tips, and much more. We are honored to assist writers expand and grow in the journey of becoming published authors.

For More Information

Creative Talents Unleashed

www.ctupublishinggroup.com

Creativetalentsunleashed@aol.com

.

Printed in Great Britain
by Amazon.co.uk, Ltd.,
Marston Gate.